Weird Animal Diets
Corpse-Eating Animals

by J. K. O'Sullivan

www.focusreaders.com

Focus Readers is distributed by North Star Editions:
sales@northstareditions.com | 888-417-0195

Produced for Focus Readers by Red Line Editorial.

Photographs ©: Shutterstock Images, cover, 1, 4, 7, 8, 11, 13, 14–15, 16, 19, 20, 27, 29; iStockphoto, 22; Louise Murray/Science Source, 25

Library of Congress Cataloging-in-Publication Data
Names: O'Sullivan, J. K., author.
Title: Corpse-eating animals / by J. K. O'Sullivan.
Description: Lake Elmo, MN : Focus Readers, [2022] | Series: Weird animal diets | Includes index. | Audience: Grades 2-3
Identifiers: LCCN 2021032048 (print) | LCCN 2021032049 (ebook) | ISBN 9781637390535 (hardcover) | ISBN 9781637391075 (paperback) | ISBN 9781637391617 (ebook) | ISBN 9781637392119 (pdf)
Subjects: LCSH: Animals--Food--Juvenile literature. | Animal behavior--Juvenile literature.
Classification: LCC QL756.5 .O88 2022 (print) | LCC QL756.5 (ebook) | DDC 591.5--dc23
LC record available at https://lccn.loc.gov/2021032048
LC ebook record available at https://lccn.loc.gov/2021032049

Printed in the United States of America
Mankato, MN
012022

About the Author

J. K. O'Sullivan is an award-winning science writer and journalist.

Table of Contents

Chapter 1

Scavengers

In an African grassland, a lion takes down a gazelle. Then the lion begins to eat. But its meal is cut short. Hyenas surround the lion. They scare the lion away. With the lion gone, the hyenas feast.

 Hyenas have strong teeth and powerful jaws. They can rip meat and crush bones.

In this example, the lion was a predator. It hunted and killed its food. The hyenas were **scavengers**. They ate food that had been killed by another animal.

Scavengers keep an area clean of dead animals. They recycle the **nutrients** from those bodies. And they prevent harmful bacteria

Did You Know?

Hyenas usually act as predators. Most of the time, they kill their own food.

 Many animals hunt when they need to and scavenge when they can.

from spreading. For these reasons, scavengers are an important part of the **food web**.

Chapter 2

Scavenging Mammals

Hyenas are well-known for being scavengers. But many meat-eating **mammals** will scavenge if given the chance. For example, coyotes live in Central and North America. They hunt rabbits and deer.

 Wolves do not prefer meat from dead animals. But they will eat it if they come across it.

But sometimes they can't find live food. Then they eat **carrion**.

Jackals live mostly in Africa. But one kind is found in Europe and Asia. Like hyenas, jackals are both predators and scavengers. They hunt for food. And they sometimes take food from other animals. For example, jackals see when a lion

Did You Know?

Jackals sometimes bury their food. This keeps other animals from scavenging it.

 Jackals do not often hunt larger animals. Instead, they hunt small animals such as baby gazelles.

makes a kill. They wait until the lion finishes eating. Then they hurry to the dead animal. They eat whatever remains.

Scavengers often are not picky eaters. They eat many different things, including carrion. This habit makes scavengers adaptable. They can more easily survive in a new environment.

For example, people build cities where animals live. Some animals cannot survive in cities. One reason is that they can't find enough food. But scavengers such as opossums and raccoons can survive. They can adapt to a changing environment.

 Opossums eat the whole animal, including the bones. Bones have nutrients opossums need.

Opossums are small mammals. They live in North America. They eat plants, animals, and trash. They also eat carrion. In fact, they eat almost anything. For this reason, opossums rarely starve to death.

Tasmanian Devils

Tasmanian devils are small mammals. They live in Tasmania. This island state is part of Australia. Tasmanian devils sleep during the day. At night, they sniff out food. Their strong sense of smell leads them to carrion. Tasmanian devils eat the whole body. They tear the meat with their sharp teeth. They crunch the bones with their strong jaws. Similar to hyenas, Tasmanian devils scavenge other animals' food. They also keep the land clean. They do this by eating old or rotten carrion.

Sharp teeth help Tasmanian devils eat carrion.

Chapter 3

Carrion-Eating Birds

Several types of birds eat carrion. For instance, vultures rarely hunt. They mostly eat carrion. Certain strengths help vultures find and eat dead animals. For example, vultures have strong eyesight.

 A flying vulture can see dead animals from 4 miles (6.4 km) away.

They can see dead or dying animals from far away. Vultures' hooked beaks are great at tearing meat.

Also, vultures have strong stomachs. Most animals cannot eat rotting meat. The bacteria in it makes them sick. But vultures' stomachs contain a powerful acid.

Did You Know?

Vultures can eat the bodies of sick animals. By doing so, they prevent the spread of deadly **diseases**.

 Turkey vultures' stomach acid is so strong it can break down metal.

It kills the bacteria. Finally, some vultures have bald heads. Vultures may get germs on their heads when they eat. But the germs don't last.

Crows sometimes eat roadkill, or the remains of animals that were killed by cars.

This is because vultures' heads have no feathers. The sun's heat can easily kill the germs.

Crows are not picky eaters. They eat fruit. They pick at trash. They hunt for insects and worms. And they steal food from other animals. Crows also eat carrion. But their beaks cannot tear through skin. So, crows wait for another animal to open a **carcass**. They eat what the animal leaves behind. Or crows wait for the carcass to **decompose**. Then the meat will be soft enough to eat.

Many other birds eat carrion when necessary. Sometimes there is no other food. For instance, ravens will eat carrion. Bald eagles will, too. Eating carrion helps them survive.

Chapter 4

Corpse-Eating Insects

Many flies eat carrion. For example, blowflies have a strong sense of smell. They can arrive at a carcass within minutes. The females lay their eggs in the body. The eggs hatch. **Larvae** come out.

 Flies gather on the corpse of a dead chick.

The larvae spit chemicals onto the flesh. The flesh turns into a liquid. The larvae drink it up. They grow and grow. Eventually, they fly away as adults.

Fly larvae are called maggots. Maggots do not eat healthy, living flesh. So, some doctors use them

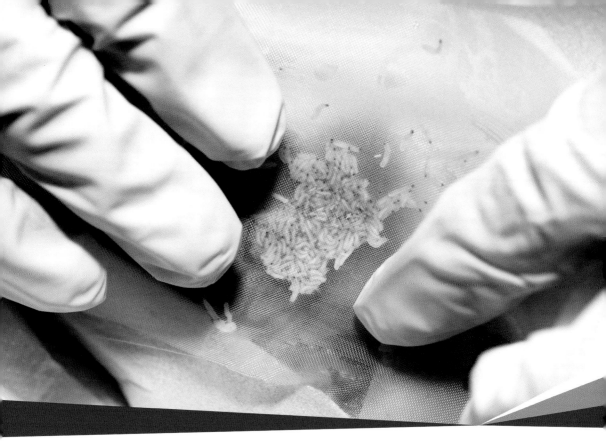

 In maggot therapy, doctors place maggots in a wound and cover it.

to treat wounds. The maggots eat the hurt flesh. They also give off a chemical. It stops bacteria from growing. The wound stays clean. It also heals faster.

Carrion beetles have a strong sense of smell. They can smell a carcass from 0.5 miles (0.8 km) away. They go to the carcass. Then they bury it. Some **species** cover the carcass in slime. The slime keeps the body from decomposing. It also hides the body's smell. That way, other beetles won't come to eat it.

Female beetles lay eggs on or near the body. After they hatch, baby beetles feast on the body.

Carrion beetles cover a dead mouse.

Corpse-eating animals break down carrion. They keep Earth clean of dead bodies. And they protect living animals from harmful bacteria. They are important members of the food web.

FOCUS ON
Corpse-Eating Animals

Write your answers on a separate piece of paper.

1. Write a sentence summarizing how scavengers are helpful for the environment.

2. Which of the corpse-eating animals were you most interested to learn about? Why?

3. What prevents vultures from being harmed by rotting meat?
   - **A.** strong eyesight
   - **B.** strong stomach acid
   - **C.** strong beaks

4. What might happen if there weren't corpse-eating animals?
   - **A.** Harmful bacteria might spread.
   - **B.** Dead animals might never decompose.
   - **C.** Animals might have more food.

5. What does **adaptable** mean in this book?

*They eat many different things, including carrion. This makes them **adaptable**. They can more easily survive in a new environment.*

  A. able to change to fit a new place
  B. able to bend over easily
  C. able to live in only one place

6. What does **starve** mean in this book?

*In fact, they eat almost anything. For this reason, opossums rarely **starve** to death.*

  A. to get better quickly
  B. to eat a lot of food
  C. to suffer from hunger

Answer key on page 32.

Glossary

carcass
The dead body of an animal.

carrion
The rotting flesh of dead animals.

decompose
To break down, become rotten, or decay.

diseases
Illnesses or sicknesses.

food web
The feeding relationships among different living things.

larvae
Insects that have hatched from eggs and are in the early stages of life.

mammals
Animals that have hair and produce milk for their young.

nutrients
Substances that living things need to stay strong and healthy.

scavengers
Animals that eat dead and decaying remains of living things.

species
Groups of animals or plants of the same kind.

To Learn More

BOOKS

Duhig, Holly. *Blood and Guts*. Minneapolis: Lerner Publications, 2020.

Halls, Kelly Milner. *Death Eaters: Meet Nature's Scavengers*. Minneapolis: Millbrook Press, 2018.

Huddleston, Emma. *Decomposers and Scavengers: Nature's Recyclers*. Minneapolis: Abdo Publishing, 2020.

NOTE TO EDUCATORS

Visit **www.focusreaders.com** to find lesson plans, activities, links, and other resources related to this title.

Index

B

bacteria, 6, 18–19, 25, 27

blowflies, 23–24

C

carrion beetles, 26

coyotes, 9–10

crows, 20–21

D

doctors, 24

F

food web, 7, 27

H

hyenas, 5–6, 9–10, 14

J

jackals, 10–11

M

maggots, 24–25

N

nutrients, 6

O

opossums, 12–13

P

predators, 6, 10

R

raccoons, 12

ravens, 21

S

scavengers, 6–7, 9–10, 12, 14

T

Tasmanian devils, 14

V

vultures, 17–20